Text by *V. M.*

Design by *Denis Lasarev*

Translated from the Russian
by *Julia Redkina*

Photography by *Roman Beniaminson,
Leonid Bogdanov, Pavel Demidov,
Vladimir Filipov, Leonard Kheifets,
Vladimir Korniushin, Vladimir Melnikov,
Yury Molodkovets, Victor Poliakov,
Nikolai Rakhmanov, Victor Savik,
Evgueny Siniaver, Vladimir Solomatin,
Vladimir Terebenin, Oleg Trubsky,
Vasily Vorontsov*

The title of Radishchev's *Journey from St Petersburg to Moscow* is familiar to every Russian. Far less known to the reader is another piece of Russian literature, *A Journey from Moscow to St Petersburg* by Alexander Pushkin who wrote in the book: "There is no truth where there is no love". These words can give the key to the understanding of the mysterious Russian soul and its everlasting search after truth which has always been and will be forever the essence of Russian life. The serene wisdom of the Russian poetical genius illuminates the course of the country's historical development. Now we invite you to make a trip to the centuries-old history of the Russian land.

Taking our way southward from the Neva and Volkhov banks we follow the ancient route "from the Varangians (Scandinavians) to the Greeks" developed in the remote past when neither Moscow nor St Petersburg existed yet. Boats loaded with all sorts of goods crossed the stormy Baltic sea, sailed down the slow northern rivers, were carried overland and then following the Neva, Volkhov, Lovat, Pripyat and Dnieper were making their way toward Kiev, "the mother of Russian towns", to go farther on across the Black Sea and Mediterranean to Constantinople (Istanbul), the capital of Byzantium, called by the Russians the "royal city". Caravans of the merchant adventurers were escorted by brave Varangian warriors who used to sing: "If you see a merchant, protect him and made him pay a tribute". Peaceful coexistence of different nations based on that commercial-military union, union of trade and military valour led to their final merging when the Varangians adopted both the religion and language of the East Slavs. In the 9th century Scandinavian prince Rurik settled first in the town of Ladoga, later moved to Novgorod and became its ruler, he was followed by his kinsman Oleg who made Kiev his capital, thus he founded the grand principality of Kiev, the forerunner of the Russian state.

A millennium has gone since the time when a small fortress of Ladoga was a busy commercial centre witnessing Slav and foreign merchants selling and buying various things at its walls. They were Finns (or rather they came from different Finnish tribes: *Ves, Vod, Izhora* and *Meria* inhabiting the territory together with the Slavs), Varangians (Scandinavians) and even Greeks, *Khazars* (Turkic people), Persians and Arabs coming here from the distant Oriental lands.

The past is alive while it is kept in our memory and we tell about it in legends, tales, songs, poems, drama and opera. That's why our trip from St Petersburg to Moscow and back from Moscow to St Petersburg will be visibly and invisibly accompanied by ancient Russian epics, Pushkin's poems, Rimsky-Korsakov's music and all of Russia's age-old cultural heritage.

St Petersburg and Moscow are two Russian capitals, two cornerstones of the Russian state, its economy, culture and science. Their rivalry has been as fruitful for Russia's development and welfare as their cooperation and union.

St Petersburg begins at its beautiful suburbs which encircle the city like a sparkling necklace of precious stones. They are famous for the former royal residences boasting both luxurious palaces and picturesque parks. Noteworthy for their historical and cultural value are Peterhof (Petrodvorets), Strelna, Tsarskoye Selo (Pushkin), Pavlovsk and Gatchina, all of which

have been retrieved from the ashes by the dextrous hands of restorers after World War II. A small town of Oranienbaum (Lomonosov) on the southern shore of the Gulf of Finland shared the fate of Leningrad (St Petersburg) and endured the enemy's 900-day siege. It was the only summer royal residence not occupied and destroyed by the Nazis. Never has the enemy set the foot on that land, neither has he on Island of Kotlin with the fortress of Kronstadt, the city's maritime outpost, and St Petersburg itself. The fortresses of Ladoga, Oreshek (Shlisselburg), Ivangorod and Izborsk are also memorials of Russian military and naval glory.

Situated in the city suburbs are numerous former country estates once owned by members of the nobility which seem to be dozing in the greenery of their parks. Visitors are attracted to their age-old alleys and calm placid lakes reflecting marble statues, grottoes, pavilions and small bridges. There, in the peace and quiet of those venerable places, best Russian music was composed, most beautiful pictures painted, deep philosophical works and great novels written. The past is eager to manifest itself to us breaking the silence and telling about the days that have gone forever.

←
On the river

Everybody is in a cheerful mood, looking forward to new impressions. The weather is calm and the sky is serene

Saint Petersburg

Desolate flat shores, featureless marshy lowlands, dense woods, poor villages with dark log cabins and frail boats of fishermen under the pale northern sky covered with low clouds – such was the territory, originally Russian, then annexed to Sweden and won back by Peter the Great where the city of St Petersburg was founded. Built to a single plan St Petersburg grew at an incredible speed as if challenging both the nature and enemies. It was named after apostle Peter, the first among the apostles. Best Western architects, engineers and artisans contributed to its construction. Here is a short chronicle of the city's history.

On May 16 (27, new style), 1707, on the day of Pentecost (feast day of the Holy Trinity in the Russian Orthodox Church), Peter the Great laid himself the foundation stone of Sts Peter and Paul's Cathedral on Zayachy Island. The date is taken as the founding date of St Petersburg. Peter visited the Island of Kotlin occupying a good strategic position in the Gulf of Finland and ordered to build there the fortress of Kronslot (later Kronstadt) to protect the city's approaches. The construction started in the winter and was completed in the May of 1704. In 1712 the capital was transferred from Moscow to St Petersburg. A number of decrees promoting the city's development were issued: stone construction was allowed nowhere in the country except St Petersburg, high officials, the royal court, members of the nobility, tradesmen and artisans were compelled to move to the new capital. In the reign of Peter II (1727) the court returned to Moscow, St Petersburg's construction halted, its population decreased and most of the noblemen left it. When Anna Ioannovna ascended the throne in 1730, she made St Petersburg the capital again and forced its settlement.

Monument to Peter the Great
(The Bronze Horseman)

Admiralty

Resurrection Church
(Church-on-the-Spilled-Blood)

St Isaac's Cathedral

→
White night. The Trinity bridge is drawn

In the reign of Empress Elizabeth, Peter the Great's daughter, the brilliant architect Rastrelli designed a great number of beautiful buildings in the Russian Baroque style – the Winter Palace, the Smolny Convent, the Stroganov Palace in Nevsky and others. At the end of her reign the population rose to 150.000 (twice as much as in Anna Ioannovna's time). Catherine the Great rather encouraged than compelled people to migrate to the city granting them privileges. She spared no expense for the city's perfection which displayed a remarkable richness of architecture. To this period belong the Holy Trinity Cathedral in St Alexander Nevsky's Monastery, the Church of the Vladimir Icon of the Most Holy Theotokos, the Marble and Tauride palaces, the Public Library and the Academy of Arts. The empress founded the Hermitage gallery and constructed its first buildings. The Neva, Fontanka and Catherine Canal were embanked with granite. At the time of Catherine the Great the population numbered 220.000. In the early 19th century when the country was ruled by Alexander I, the city was embellished with the Cathedral of the Kazan Icon of the Most Holy Theotokos, the General Headquarters building, the Mikhailovsky Palace (now, the Russian Museum), the Admiralty, the Stock Exchange and many others.

In 1861 Alexander II abolished serfdom which gave another impact to the city's growth and development. Greater mobility of labour was allowed and after 1890 the population began to increase rapidly. Before World War I it numbered 1.500.000, a lot of new factories opened, there was much industrial growth in the city.

In its early days St Petersburg became a major cultural and industrial centre, the cradle of Russian science. First merchantmen and warships were built in its shipyards. Established here were the first public museum *Kunstkammer* (Chamber

White night.
View of St Petersburg's central part

Statue of the River Neva
decorating a Rostral Column

Sts Peter and Paul's Cathedral

Interior of Sts Peter and Paul's Cathedral

Tombstone of Peter the Great

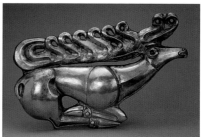

of Curiosity), the Academy of Science, St Petersburg University, the Public (now, Russian National) Library and a first observatory. The city flourished: magnificent granite embankments had replaced the marshy banks, the streets were paved and the palaces rivalled each other in grandeur.

Most important inventions in physics and chemistry have been made in the city laboratories, the first plane constructed and space research started. St Petersburg saw the Golden age of Russian literature as its most celebrated names were associated with the city. It is a focus of rail routes, their lines carry 6.000.000 passengers a year. There are five principal rail terminals in it.

St Petersburg has changed its name thrice: in 1914 into Petrograd, in 1924 into Leningrad and in 1991 reverted to St Petersburg. It spreads across 42 islands. 65 rivers and canals spanned by 600 bridges flow through the city. In the west it is washed by the Gulf of Finland with the coastline 40 km long. Its total area is 600 km², the population numbers 5.000.000. 5% of Russia's industrial output is produced here.

St Petersburg's history has been dramatic, sometimes even tragic, yet great.

Palace Square. The Winter Palace and the Alexander Column

Jordan Staircase in the Winter Palace

Atlantes at the New Hermitage entrance

Peacock *clock*

Deer. *Scythian gold*

Venus of Tauris

Leonardo da Vinci. Madonna Litta

Raphael's loggias

Knights' room

Peter the Great's memorial room

Renoir. Child with a Whip

Picasso. Boy with a Dog

Boudoir

In the 900-day siege (1941–44) the city lost almost a million people who died from starvation and shelling. The city defended fiercely and did not surrender. Completely restored after the war, it is as beautiful and majestic as ever.

St Petersburg stretches along the banks of the Neva, its main waterway and favourite sight of both Petersburgers and visitors. No wonder, "the regal coursing" of the river, which is only 74 km long, has inspired poets, musicians and artists. It issues from Ladoga near the town of Shlisselburg (Oreshek), forms a semicircle and discharges into the Gulf of Finland. The city lies on the wide delta between the Neva arms.

The Bolshaya (Great) Neva is spanned by eight bridges within the historical centre. One of the most majestic is the ten-span Trinity Bridge (580 m long, 24 m wide) designed by engineers from the French firm *Batignol* who had won an international competition for the project. The longest is St Alexander Nevsky's Bridge (906 m long) lying upstream.

This grandiose ferro-concrete structure faced with granite was designed by local engineers in 1960–65. The ninth bridge across the river is situated in the outer city where the frontline was laid in the days of World War II. *Nevsky piatachek* is a small patch of land all covered with the blood of the soldiers who defended the approaches to Leningrad (St Petersburg). So cruel and bloody were the battles that even today, almost sixty years later, grass doesn't grow there.

The Neva is so deep that during the last war submarines and ocean liners could reach St Petersburg and were moored at its embankments. The full-flowing river looks calm but it can be very dangerous. The city is subject to flooding especially in autumn and early winter. All in all there have been 300 floods in its history, exceptionally severe inundations occurred in 1723, November 23, 1824, November 7 and 1924, September 24.

To control the destructive floodwaters the city began construction of a dike across the Gulf of Finland. It has joined its western shore and the Island of Kotlin where the Kronstadt fortress stands. The Neva links the Gulf of Finland to the basins of Ladoga, Onega, Beloye and Ilmen lakes. The Volga-Baltic Canal system (former Mariinsky) joins the river to the Volga, which makes it an important waterway.

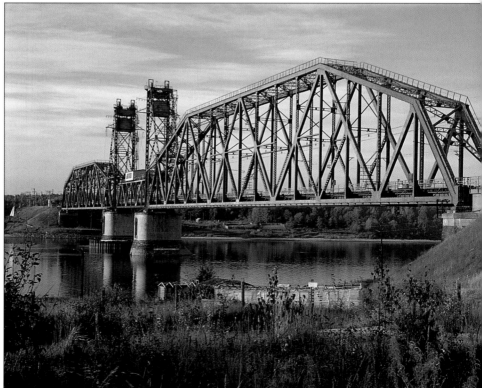

River station

Church on the site of the Neva battle. Here, at the confluence of the Neva and the Izhora, St Alexander Nevsky defeated the Swedes in 1240

Neva River outside the city. Quiet green banks

Finland Railway Bridge across the Neva

→

Oreshek Fortress (later developed into the town of Shlisselburg) stands at the place where the Neva flows out of Ladoga Lake

Ladoga Lake is the largest in Europe, twice as large as Onega, five times larger than Chudskoye and ten times larger than Saimaa to say nothing of smaller Western lakes. It is 18.000 km^2 in area, with a maximum length of 219 km, an average width of 83 km and an average depth of 50 m. Its boundless space looks like a sea, no shores are visible from its open part. The depression of the lake was produced by the action of glaciers, that's why seals still live here.

Many rivers and streams empty into Ladoga while only the Neva issues from it. Its south-eastern shores are low and regular, with no islands nearby. The north-western part that we are bound for has numerous islands fringing the shores which are high, craggy and broken by deep fjord-like inlets. The islands that echo in their shape the line of the shores form reefs. They are strikingly beautiful with their high sheer granite rocks sharply rising above the water. Coniferous trees grow on them stretching out their branches to the dim sun of the north.

Many quarries have been active on the northern shores. Granite obtained there was used for St Petersburg's construction. When Leningrad (St Petersburg) was under siege by the Germans (1941–44), Ladoga Lake was the lifeline connecting it with the rest of the country. Supplies and military equipment were brought to the city and the sick were evacuated from it across the water and ice. Today ships and boats conveying passengers from St Petersburg to Nizhny Novgorod and Astrakhan and tourists to Valaam and the fortress of Oreshek cross Ladoga Lake.

Located in the centre of the lake's northern part is the archipelago consisting of fifty islands and named after the biggest of them Valaam. There on the high cliffs stands the Valaam Transfiguration Monastery, a major place of pilgrimage in Russia, a realm of elders and ascetics, a land steeped in holiness. The monastery founded in the 10th century is stauropegial, which means that it is directly guided by the Patriarch of Moscow and All Russia (not by a local bishop). The name of Valaam can be translated from Finnish as "the high land". Sometimes the name of the island is attributed to the biblical prophet Balaam or, more likely, to the Slav pagan idol Baal (Veles, Volos). One of Valaam legends says that a long time ago the island used to be a huge site of pagan sacrifices.

The total area of the Valaam archipelago is 36 km, with a maximum length of 13 and 8 km. Its rocky islands are covered with coniferous woods, picturesque grasslands and green meadows. It is the place where the God-created beauty of the islands and the man-made beauty of architecture and art blend harmoniously. The imposing blue cathedral domes of the monastery located in the southern part of the island near the Monastery Bay can be seen from almost any point.

Some of the Valaam islands are joined by bridges. There are nine small lakes in the main island of the archipelago. Straits, bays, lakes surrounded by thick plants and sullen granite rocks reflect everything in their azure... The harmony of the archipelago is evident to everyone.

The nature of Valaam is unique. The monks did not cut down trees, they used for construction and heating only fallen ones. There are no large beasts here but one can encounter hares, foxes, squirrels and elks which are not afraid of people because they have never been hunted.

Valaam separated by nature from secular settlements is an ideal place for

Holy gate

Transfiguration Monastery

At the monastery wall

→
St Nicholas' Skete

monastic life and solitude, as if especially destined to glorify God. Austere, almost vertical rocky shores, like sullen granite walls, rise as high as 50 m above sea-level.

According to tradition, the monastery was established in 992 by the Greek monks Sergius and Herman (canonized by the Russian Orthodox Church) who came here seeking solitude for their ascetic endeavours. Over and over again the monastery was destroyed. Located on the border of the Novgorod-the-Great lands and Sweden it was ravaged by the Swedes several times. In 1611 they alighted at Valaam for the last time and gave everything to fire and sword. The island remained deserted until 1715 when the monastery was revived by Peter the Great. Russian emperors Alexander I, Alexander II and Nicholas II came to venerate this sacred place. Most of the elegant monastery structures date from the 19th century. The heart of the cloister is the Transfiguration Cathedral (1887–96) designed by Karpov and other architects. Another marvellous construction is St Nicholas' Church in the skete of the same name by Gornostayev. The monastery was a source of inspiration for many well-known figures of Russian culture, the poet Tiutchev, composer Tchaikovsky and painter Shishkin among them. The long austere service sung in plaintive ancient Znamenny chant bespoke the timelessness of eternity. The church glowed in the light of a thousand of candles and the icons reflected the uncreated light that emanated from the rites and the mysteries.

After the revolution of 1917 Finland gained independence and Valaam became part of its territory. About 200 monks led an ascetic life on Valaam at that time. They lived in prayer and ascetic labour. The monastery had different workshops: a smithy, carpenter's, candle-making

Pine-trees on top of rocks

Road amid rocks

Ships are resting

Gate of the Skete of All Saints

Sheer granite rocks

factory, icon-painting studio, photographer's, diary farm, library, printing house, shipyard and shoe-maker's. Monks were also occupied in wood-carving, fishing and gardening. Though the climate of Valaam is harsh, the monastery gardens yielded large crops, even water-melons and pumpkins grew here. The monastery farm produced milk, butter and cheese for both monks and pilgrims.

In 1940 Valaam became the Soviet territory. The monks had to move to Finland where they founded the New Valaam cloister. They took with them the monastery library consisting of 30.000 books. During World War II the archipelago was occupied by the Finns. In the days of the war Valaam was bombarded but the damage was not serious, Sts Sergius and Herman protected their monastery. Only the ruins of the Finnish officers' club, some fortifications and a canteen reminded of those days. After the war the monastery was used as a boarding house for disabled soldiers and elderly people.

In 1986 the Metropolitan of Leningrad Alexius (now Patriarch of All Russia) consecrated the Transfiguration Cathedral given back to the Church and in 1989 monastic life resumed here. In 1992 most of the clerical and administrative buildings were returned to the monastery. However the main monastic aim is not the restoration of the walls but rising a man in Christ's spirit, living in patience and keeping clear conscience.

Thousands of tourists and pilgrims come to Valaam. The sky seems closer to one standing on its hills. "Let God give you what you are seeking here!", said one schemamonk to the popular Russian writer Ivan Shmelev who visited the island in the early 20th century.

St Nicholas' Skete

Resurrection Skete

Granite cross (1861) with the symbols of Orthodox Christianity and Christ's passions

The Svir unites two biggest lakes in Europe, Onega and Ladoga, it issues from the former and empties into the latter. The river which is 224 km long is a part of the White Sea-Baltic and Volga-Baltic Canal systems. Two hydroelectric stations are active on it, one upstream and the other downstream. The Svir banks are marvellous in their diversity: sheer and covered with woods or crowned with red vertical rocks alternating with green velvet marshes. For a long time these lands were wild and thinly-populated. During the Mongol invasion people fled to towns, not to dense woods. In 1487 the monk Alexander from the Valaam Monastery (canonized by the Russian Church) came to these parts and founded a cloister here which is known now as St Alexander Svirsky's Monastery. It was destroyed by the Swedes in 1561, the Poles

and Lithuanians in 1613 and the Soviets after 1917. The cloister is being restored now. The holy relics of its founder have been recently found in a museum and translated to the monastery. Today monasticism seems obscure to many people. The cause of a monk is prayer: for those who close and those who are far away, for those who hate and those who love, for the whole world corrupted by sin, the world which is probably still alive only thanks to the prayers of the righteous men.

The Svir provides the country with good timber floated by local inhabitants downstream and stored there. The river is abundant in fish, especially salmon and trout. It is not, however, very good for navigation as it is not deep (up to 5 m in autumn) but meandrous, has rapids and is often fogbound. All these factors, however, don't hinder courageous and experienced captains safely steering their ships up- and downstream.

A small town of Svirstroy with a population of 1.5 thousand (on the left bank) and the Nizhnesvirskaya hydroelectric power station were built simultaneously. The Svir was canalized, most dangerous of its rapids inundated, which made the river navigable. The station is located on a small island in the middle of the dam that is 30 m high and 1.5 km long.

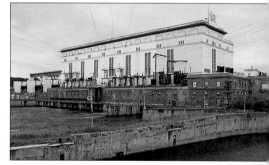

Village on the River Svir

Country church

Nizhnesvirskaya hydroelectric station

These small fur-trees will grow big...

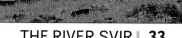

MANDROGA

A small village of Mandroga is a romantic vision from the past. Similar log cabins are to be seen in Pavlovsk near St Petersburg – the restaurant *Podvorye*. Both "villages" have been recently created by men of enterprise and artistic taste as tourist attractions. Their cosy log cabins designed in old Russian style attract visitors who can enjoy here the fanciful wood-carving, visit a museum of samovars, buy some souvenirs made by local craftsmen and have a good meal with Russian vodka or tea.

The history of the place is not so romantic. There used to be a settlement of *Veps* (Karelian people). In the days of the last war it was occupied by the Germans, the population was interned never to return and the place became desolate. In the 1960s sand was obtained here but the workers left the village when the quarries were closed. Today the population is small, yet industrious and enterprising. The head of the community says there are some *Veps* (descendants of the natives) among them. Mandroga means "pine-trees on the bog" in the *Veps* language. The local people are not cast down, they are working hard and feel hopeful about the future.

Another attraction is the Museum of Vodka. This traditional Russian alcoholic drink is made of grain. Many dishes of Russian cuisine can be washed down with vodka, like pan cakes and caviar. The museum exhibitions show the history of the drink and the process of its production. There is a tasting bar where the visitors can taste best sorts of Russian vodka.

Exhibition of samovars

Wood-carving decorating the windows of Mandroga

Village. At dinner

Our ship enters Onega, the second largest lake in Europe after Ladoga. It is an enormous freshwater reservoir. The southern shores are regular, low and often marshy. The shores to the north are high and rocky, overgrown with forest and have deep, narrow bays looking like fjords. The lake has the shape of a crayfish, or lobster, with raised claws. It is almost 30 m deep, the depth in the hollows is 120 m. More than fifty rivers and numerous streams empty into Onega with only the Svir issuing from it. Some historical documents mention that pearl-oysters were found in the rivers flowing into Onega Lake. The pearls had a regular spherical form and were of pure silvery-white colour. They were considered of much value. Nowadays they are extremely rare. The lake of Onega has about 1.300 islands, mostly in the northern part. It contains more than 40 species of fish including salmon and trout, the latter is artificially bred, as it actually comes from Sevan Lake in Armenia. 200 species of birds nest on Onega's shores, there are wild ducks, geese, swans and cranes. Its forests are inhabited by bears, deer, wolves, foxes and even musk rats whose native land is Northern America.

Many historical sites are to be found on the shores of the lake. One of them is Demons' (Besov) Cape situated in the lake's eastern part, not far from the town of Pudozh. It is formed by a cliff, 40 m high. The cape is two km long. In the 19th century numerous petroglyphs dating from the 3rd millennium B.C. were discovered here. The monks of the Murom Monastery located not far from the place called them "demons' prints", hence the name of the cape. They even tried to destroy them. Today the cape contains more than a thousand of carvings. Another attraction is the Transfiguration Cathedral

Tavern

Treating to a glass of vodka and traditional Russian fare: pickled cucumbers, onions, leeks, garlic, bacon and salt. Only rye bread is lacking

Exhibition of samovars. You can not only look at them but also have a cup of tea which has a special taste when made in a samovar

on Kizhi island. This elegant structure crowned with twenty-two cupolas is a real masterpiece of Russian wooden architecture. Noteworthy are houses and chapels decorated with fine wood-carving which are to be seen in many villages situated on the lake shores.

The climate is so cold that cabbages, onions, buckwheat and oats which used to be the main foodstuff for the Russians don't grow here. The life of a peasant in this region was very hard. He earned his living mainly from fishing in Onega which was abundant in fish. Fish was sold to St Petersburg and other towns so the Onega population made contacts with the rest of the country. Lands to the north and the east of Onega are swampy and covered with endless forests, that's why a cart, a traditional vehicle of peasants, could not run there. Even in summer local people used sledges pulled by horses or simply rode horses. During long northern winters when it grew dark early peasants told legends and sang *byliny* (narrative poetry transmitted orally). The oldest of them dealt with the Golden age of Kievan Rus, the deeds of Prince Vladimir the Red Sun and the warrior Ilya of Murom who defended Russia from the enemy.

Bitterly cold are winters here with strong icy winds and much snow, autumns are astonishingly colourful and on bright summer days the cupolas of magnificent old Russian churches attract hosts of visitors.

A small island, 8 km long and less than 1.5 km wide, is washed by the Onega waters. Its elevated central part forms a ridge dividing the island into two, the wider and lower western and narrower eastern parts. It is mostly covered with meadows, a thin forest belt borders its shores, there are also marshes with willow bushes. Great elm-trees feature the scenery.

The name of Kizhi island originates from the Karelian word *kizharsuari* ("island of games"). In the remote past it was a site of pagan practices that's why it was settled very early. In the 14th century Novgorod merchants stopped here on their way to the White Sea where they bought furs and walrus bone articles.

The first Christian settlement was formed around the Saviour Church in the 16th century. It developed into a major religious centre with the diocese including 120 villages and hamlets. Later it served as a defence outpost. There are some old engravings showing fortifications on the island of which only the brick foundation, restored in 1959, is extant.

The Livonian war, in the reign of Ivan the Terrible, didn't spare the island. During the Northern war it suffered from the Swedes' severe attacks. The Russian victory in that war was commemorated by construction of the Transfiguration Church. The nine-cupola Intercession Church was built half a century later, in 1764. A bell tower with the tent-shaped roof was added to it in 1874. During the reign of Catherine II several major peasant revolts took place in Kizhi between 1769 and 1774.

Twenty two cupolas
of the Transfiguration Cathedral

Village in the north

Women threading beads

Fishermen's boats
are waiting for their owners

→
Kizhi. The Transfiguration Cathedral
(a summer church without stove heating)
to the left and the Church of the Intercession
of the Most Holy Theotokos (a winter church
with stove heating) to the right

The island's main architectural landmark is the Transfiguration Church built in 1714, without a single nail. (The few nails you can see today remain from the restoration work done in the 1960s.) This strikingly beautiful structure crowned with 22 cupolas seems to be hovering in the air in any weather, whether the lake is calm and peaceful and its surface smooth or it is rough and the waves violently break on the shore. The church cupolas made of aspen wood gleam in the sunlight in daytime and the moonlight at night.

On the island...

View from the porch

Wood-carvers

The structure looks even more impressive if you believe a popular legend that it was built by one man and with one tool which was an axe. Upon affixing a final shingle, the master, whose name was Nestor, hurled the axe into the lake pronouncing that there had never been and wouldn't ever be such a thing. The Transfiguration Church houses a fine collection of iconostases (altar screens).

In 1951 the island became an open-air museum of old Russian wooden architecture. Best wooden constructions have been transferred here from nearby and distant villages. Noteworthy is St Lazarus' Church which, according to legend, was built by the monk Lazarus, the founder of the Murom monastery. He died in 1391, which means that it is the oldest wooden church extant in Russia. It is very small: the nave is only 3 m long while the porch and altar part are simply tiny. Other relics of the past located here are two wooden houses, two windmills and traditional Russian bathhouses which stand on the shore.

Russian church feasts are traditionally celebrated in Kizhi. They include Easter (Resurrection of Christ), the day of the apostles Peter and Paul (July 12), the day of the prophet Elijas (August 2), the Transfiguration of Our Lord (August 19) and some others. Kizhi has churches dedicated to all of these feasts.

In summer-time exhibitions of crafts, performances of the museum folk group and concerts of bell chimes are held on the island which was inscribed on the UNESCO world cultural and natural heritage list in 1990.

Now we are leaving Onega and making our way to the Rybinsk reservoir's northern shore by the Volga-Baltic Canal built in 1964 to replace the antiquated Mariinsky Canal system, when going through its locks became dangerous and took much time and effort.

By the window

Windmill transferred from a nearby village

Summer folk festival

The Kovzha is the name for three rivers in the north-west of Russia. We are following the most important of them which is the western Kovzha. It issues from Kovzha Lake in the Vologda province and discharges into Beloye Lake. The river is navigable and together with the Sheksna makes a part of the Volga-Baltic waterway.

Its original length was about 107 km, but after the construction of the Volga-Baltic Canal its bed has been changed. In the northern part the river flows in its original bed (43 km long), its almost vertical banks with precipitous rocks are very picturesque.

Kovzha. Landing stage

Sails have been furled.
When the wind fails, a motor can be used

Beloye (White) Lake situated in the north of the Vologda province covers an area of 1.400 km but its average depth is less than 4 m. The Sheksna enters it and the Kovzha issues from it. The lake and rivers form a part of the Volga-Baltic waterway.

Modern scholars consider the name a derivation from the language of the local *Veps* who called it "a white lake". However the *Geographical Dictionary of Russia* published in 1801 says: "It (the lake) is rather deep with pure and clear water, the bottom is stony in some places but mostly clayey. The clay is of white colour and when, in stormy weather, it is mixed with the water the latter also changes its colour into white."

The lake's shape used to be oval, but has been changed by the Volga-Baltic Canal construction which increased its water level. It has a sandy bottom with stony shoals near the northern shores. It is not very deep but there are some deep hollows in it. Its low shores overgrown with

forest are marshy and abundant in grasslands. Strong winds blowing here made the navigation extremely dangerous, especially for smaller boats, so a bypass canal was dug along its southern shore in 1818. Now the lake is included into the Volga-Baltic waterway. It is rich in fish, particularly pike, perch, eel-pout, beam, roach, sterlet (small sturgeon) and smelt which is most popular.

Since ancient times Beloye Lake with its rivers has been connecting the north with the south. In the early 20th century it became part of the Mariinsky Canal replaced by the Volga-Baltic waterway which has damaged its ecological system:

Kovzha. Forest bordering the shore is reflected in the smooth surface of the lake

River buoy shows a navigable channel to the ships and boats

some of the forests have been inundated and are decaying in water. An ecological station controlling the process is active in the town of Belozersk.

Russian folklore contains many songs, *byliny* and legends about Beloye Lake and the town of Belozersk located on its southern shore. Founded very early, before Prince Rurik, Belozersk was originally a settlement of the local *Veps* people. It became desolated after the plague of the 14th century. The modern town is situated at a distance of 18 km from its ancient site. In 1487 it was turned into a defence outpost on the northern border of Russia and became the main town of the Belozersk principality which was later annexed to Moscow after all of its princes had perished in the battle of Kulikovo.

Earthen ramparts and wooden walls with eight towers were built here in the 15th century. The walls were demolished in the late 17th century while the ramparts are still extant. The five-cupola Transfiguration Cathedral (1668–70) is located in the centre of the town within the territory surrounded with old earthen ramparts. The ditch around it is spanned by a long stone bridge constructed in the 18th century which joins it with the rest of the town. The interior of the cathedral displays a lavish wood-carving decor. Its iconostasis is adorned with gilded wooden sculpture. The magnificent arc above the altar table and gorgeous icon-cases are also made of wood and painted or gilded. Belozersk boasts many 17th- and 18th-century buildings as well as some Classical mansions dating from the 19th century. Other noteworthy architectural features are the old trading arcade and the Assembly of the Nobility building. The Belozersk museum of folk and applied arts shows a collection of 18th-century icons, a gallery of 18th- and 19th-century paintings and fine samples of local pottery and embroidery.

Beloye (White) Lake. Pine-trees and seagulls above the water surface

Foggy morning on Beloye Lake

Tug in the Volga-Baltic Canal

Goritsy, a village on the eastern bank of the Sheksna River, is famous for the Resurrection Convent which has been recently returned to the Russian Orthodox Church. Damaged in the Soviet period it is being restored now. Its holy spring attracts pilgrims. The cloister was founded by Euphrosyne, the spouse of Prince Andrew, Ivan III's son. Accused of being implicated in the plot against the tsar she was exiled to Goritsy and compelled to take the veil. Her son Vladimir whom the boyars had intended to enthrone was executed in Moscow. Euphrosyne (Eudoxia in monasticism) was accompanied by some of her needlewomen who organized a workshop of handicrafts here. Eudoxia's embroidery is exhibited in the Museum of St Cyril's Monastery. In the Time of Troubles Princess Xenia, Boris Godunov's daughter, was kept here. In 1730 Catherine Dolgoruky, Peter II's bride, was brought to the convent. Many of the Goritsy nuns were of noble birth. Mother Pheophany Gotovtseva, the first abbess of the Novodevichy Convent in St Petersburg, took the veil here.

The oldest structure is the cubical Resurrection Church put up in 1544. Adjacent to it is the Church of St Demetrius (1611). The 17th-century bell tower has also been preserved. The Trinity Cathedral and convent walls date back to the 19th century.

Traditional food of the Russian north is sold at an open-air market in Goritsy, including dried fish, mushrooms and greens as well as flowers.

Goritsy. The Resurrection Convent.
A holy spring to the left of the boat.
The cloister is being restored

At the landing stage. Souvenirs
made by local craftsmen are sold here

In Goritsy

Flowers, mushrooms
and dried fish are on sale.
You may choose whatever you want

KIRILLOV

At a distance of 8 km from Goritsy there lies the town of St Cyril – Kirillov (a bus goes there). It is an important port in the Severo-Dvinsk waterway and one of the largest towns in the Vologda province. Main industries are timber working and food procession. The town is a major historical and cultural site inscribed on the list of most important historical places. It was formed round the St Cyril of Beloye Lake Monastery, a second largest cloister in the north, after the Solovki Monastery in the White Sea. Its founder and first abbot St Cyril (1337–1427) was the son of a boyar and took monastic vows when he was not young. Once he heard the voice: "Go to the lake and you'll find peace and salvation there." He prayed all night long and went to the north. Led by the Divine Providence he found a place on the lake shore where he established a monastery.

A lot of new monasteries opened in the country in the late 14th century which was a period of great spiritual and patriotic upsurge. In 1380 the Russians defeated the Mongols at the battle of Kulikovo demonstrating the developing independence of the Russian lands from the Mongol rule. St Sergius of Radonezh, who reconciled conflicting Russian princes and is revered as the saint protector of Russia, had blessed Prince Dimitry Donskoy for the battle and predicted his victory. St Cyril was one of St Sergius' followers.

He lived his first year here, in the north, in complete solitude. Later he built the Dormition Church (now the Dormition Cathedral). Its main icon was painted by

Fortified wall of St Cyril's Monastery facing Siverskoye Lake

Dormition Monastery. Holy Gate (1323) and Church of St John Climacus (1575)

Fortified wall

Church of the Entry into the Temple with a refectory (1519), a bell tower (1761) and the churches of Gabriel the Archangel and St Cyril (both, 1780)

→

St Cyril's Monastery as viewed from Siverskoye Lake. In the Time of Troubles the Polish invaders tried to storm the monastery from this point, but all their attempts failed

the famous icon-painter Andrei Rublev. St Cyril died at the age of 90. At that time there were 35 monks in the cloister.

The monastery with its churches, chapels and administrative buildings which had been created for some centuries turned into a major place of pilgrimage. In 1529 Grand Prince Vasily and his wife Helen Glinsky prayed here asking God to give them a son. A year later Ivan IV (Ivan the Terrible) was born. In commemoration of the event the churches of Gabriel the Archangel and St John the Baptist were erected. Tsar Ivan supported the cloister. He visited it four times and when living here, kept all the monastery rules. In the early 17th century the monastery owned much land and 600 villages. In 1612 it was besieged by the Poles who were routed by the monks and soldiers. Later the tsar ordered to fortify the monastery so that it would protect the Russian borders from the Swedes and it turned into an impregnable fortress with the walls, 11 m high. The disgraced Patriarch Nicon whose reforms had caused a schism in the Church was sent here in 1676. In Catherine II's reign the monastery fell into a decline, only 33 monks lived in it.

In 1919 its property was nationalized and in 1924 it was closed. Its premises were given to an orphanage. Only in 1968 a first exhibition of old Russian art was opened in it which later developed into a museum. Now it is still used by the museum though some of the buildings have been transmitted to the Church.

Monastery of St John the Baptist.
A stone arc over the chapel and cross were made by St Cyril himself.
Church of St John the Baptist is to the right

Church of St Sergius of Radonezh and a refectory adjacent to it

Old frescoes at the monastery entrance

Icon of St Cyril with the scenes of his life. Early 16th century

Icon of the Dormition of the Most Holy Theotokos. Early 15th century. Museum of St Cyril's Monastery

Icon of the Saviour. Ca. 1497. Museum of St Cyril's Monastery

The Severo-Dvinsk waterway starts from the Sheksna reservoir near the village of Topornia. It follows some canals, lakes and rivers, crosses Kubenskoye Lake and then by the Sukhona flows into the Severnaya Dvina. The canal system, 135 km long, includes six reservoirs and eight dams. It was designed and built under the supervision of Duke Alexander of Wurtemmberg, a brother of Empress Maria Feodorovna, Paul I's spouse. Construction began in 1825 and three years later the canal system was opened for navigation.

The Sheksna in the Vologda province runs from Beloye Lake to the Volga, or the Rybinsk reservoir to be exact. The river, 164 km long, is a part of the Volga-Baltic Canal system. It was once known for its fisheries. The banks are low and covered with grasslands or marshy. The name originates from Finnish and means "a sedgy stream". It has been a link between the Russian north and the Volga since the times of Kievan Rus. At the river source there are the ruins of a church — almost nothing remains from the ancient town of Belozero, later the village of Krokhino. In the course of construction of the Volga-Baltic waterway the Sheksna has been canalized (straightened, deepened and widened) as a result the scenery has changed.

The industrial town of Cherepovets lies on the river. Its port cranes and factory chimneys can be seen from the boat. Cherepovets spreads on both banks joined by a huge bridge, 1 km long. It is suspended with steel cable and supported by the pier rooted 85 m deep under

Sheksna River

the water. The arch span is so high that all types of ships can go under it. There are many old ferries on the river, which is a charming view.

Cherepovets is noted for its large-scale ferrous metallurgy. Its iron is exported to many countries. It is also a major producer of steel in Russia. Unfortunately its industries affect the environment. The situation is aggravated by the fact the industrial part and residential section are merged and have no protection zone between them.

Noteworthy historical features are the Resurrection Cathedral in the late Baroque style (1752), Classical mansions of merchants from the early 19th century and wooden houses from the second half of the 19th century.

Another feature is the Church of the Nativity of Christ situated not far from the bridge across the Sheksna. Services are read here regularly.

The town has an old park laid out in 1894 which is a national preserve.

The local lore museum has celebrated its centenary. The collection was founded in 1895 and displayed in a museum building in 1898. It contains good archaeological collections, old Russian icons, applied art objects, manuscripts and old books.

In 1984 a memorial house of the Vereshchagin family was opened in the town. Most part of its exhibits deal with the life and work of the famous historical painter Vasily Vereshschagin. Trained as a naval officer and having been a direct participant in many battles where he distinguished himself by his unusual bravery, in his works he told the cruel truth about war. In April 1904 he perished near Port Arthur on the battleship *Petropavlovsk* during the Russo-Japanese War of 1904–05. Other exhibits are dedicated to his elder brother Nikolai who was an initiator and promoter of cheese and butter industrial production in Russia.

Well-known poet from the so-called Silver age of Russian literature Igor Severianin (1887–1941) spent his childhood and went to college in Cherepovets.

A small town of Sheksna, lying 55 km downstream, stretches for 7 km along the river. It is famous for good timber of which musical instruments are made and high-quality linen. The first dam of its hydroelectric power station was built in 1963 and the second in 1992. The difference in the two water levels is 13 m, the water area is 260 m by 17.5 m in the first station and 310 m by 21.5 m in the second one.

The Rybinsk reservoir was formed by two dams on the Volga and the Sheksna. This large artificial lake which developed in 1941–47 has an area of 4.580 km², a volume of 25 km³ and an average depth of 5.6 m. The lake is 140 km long and 70 km wide.

In the past the Volga, the Sheksna and the Mologa were linked by the old, rather shallow Mariinsky Canal system constructed in the first half of the 19th century. Before that, in the early 18th century, Peter the Great who had built the Ladoga by-pass Canal and Vyshny Volochek Canal system had intended to join the Kovzha and the Vytegra, which was not done then. Construction of the Mariinsky Canal began in the reign of Paul I and was completed in 1808 when Alexander I ruled Russia. Navigation was very dangerous, particularly in Beloye and Onega lakes, so by-pass canals were dug in 1852. The locks were inconvenient, as the water level was low. Sometimes boats had to be pulled or carried overland from one lock to another. A trip from St Petersburg to Rybinsk could take up to three months.

Reconstruction of the antiquated Mariinsky system started just before World

Misty morning forecasts a sunny day

Haystack

Volna (Wave) *tug ploughing through the river*

Sailing boat in the Volga-Baltic Canal

War II and finished only in 1964 when it was completely replaced by the Volga-Baltic waterway, 1.100 km long. It starts at the Rybinsk reservoir and goes northward by way of the Sheksna River to Lake Beloye, crossing the lake it follows the Kovzha and the Vytegra rivers, continues through the Onega Canal, the Svir River to Ladoga and the Novoladozhsky Canal and then to the Neva.

Although construction of the dams and enormous reservoirs have made a major contribution to the economy, it also has had adverse ecological consequences. Hundreds of villages have been completely or partly flooded. The ancient town of Mologa with its beautiful churches, cosy houses and peaceful graveyards rests on the bottom of the artificial lake. Its princes were once comrades-in-arms of Dmitry Donskoy and did much for Russia. Now Mologa's bell tower rising above the Rybinsk reservoir surface is a mournful sight.

In the distant past oriental peoples called the great Russian river *Ra* and in the middle ages the name of the river was *Itil*. The modern name is a derivation from some Finno-Ugric language. It means "white" in the languages of *Veps, Votic, Izhora (Ingra)* and other nations inhabiting the Volga region for centuries, so the "Volga" can be translated as "a river with clear water".

It is the continent's longest full-flowing river, 3.700 km long. Its basin, 1.360 km², sprawls across about two-fifth of the European part of Russia. Rising in the Valdai Hills, not far from Tver, it crosses the European part of Russia from north to south and discharges into the Caspian Sea.

Country church flooded by the Volga-Baltic Canal construction

Rybinsk reservoir. Navigation mark

In the middle of the river. There used to be a hilltop…

Boat is ready to sail

→
Volga River near Rybinsk. The Transfiguration Cathedral (19th century)

The river forms a wide delta, receiving the water of some 200 tributaries (long rivers, small streams and brooks).

The Volga basin produces 25 % of all Russia's crops and one fifth of industrial fishing. The river contains 70 species of fish, including 40 industrial (roach, herring, bream, pike-perch, wild carp, silurus, pike, sturgeon, sterlet and others).

The Volga has always been a major trading route connecting the north with the south. It is navigable from the town of Rzhev downstream. In the town of Tver it is 200 m wide. There are 40 cities and towns including Tver, Rybinsk, Yaroslavl, Kostroma, Nizhny Novgorod, Kazan, Ulianovsk, Cheboksary, Samara, Saratov, Volgograd (Stalingrad, Tsaritsyn before 1917) and Astrakhan as well as 1.000 smaller settlements on the Volga, most of which lie on the high right bank.

A string of reservoirs built in the Soviet period line the Volga, among them Volzhskoye (the Moscow Sea), Uglich, Rybinsk and others. There are six hydroelectric stations. The river is joined by canals to the Baltic, White, Azov and Black seas. It carries construction and raw materials, petroleum, foodstuffs (bread, fruits) and salt.

The French novelist Jules Verne who wrote about journeys and voyages and made them in his imagination compares the river with a great tree whose branches (arms) reach to all parts of Russia. Numerous songs, folk tales, legends, poems and even novels are dedicated to the Volga. The Russians call it "the Mother Volga" or "bread-winner" and describe it as wide, mighty, glorious, great or sometimes calm and clear.

The river unites different nations that have been living on its banks in peace

for ages: the Russians, Tartars, *Mari,*
Mordvin, Chuvash and even Germans
(Volga Germans).

Everyone in Russia knows the names of
the Volga towns and cities that didn't
surrender to the enemies in different
periods of the country's history and
where the enemies were routed. One
of the decisive battles of World War II
took place on the river, that was the
battle of Stalingrad.

Panoramic view of the Volga banks

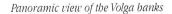

*Statue of the Volga River
at the entrance to the Rybinsk lock*

Tolga Convent near Yaroslavl

Yaroslavl

Yaroslavl is one of the oldest and most well-known of Russian provincial cities. A prosperous mercantile centre in the past, the city boasts a plethora of dazzling churches and a lovely river front aspect. Yaroslavl is a big port and a focus of rail routes. It has a population of 627.000. Its industries produce heavy machinery (diesel engines and electrical equipment), textiles and tyres. The city has a number of higher education institutes, such as medical, pedagogic and technological.

Though Yaroslavl was first mentioned in chronicles in 1071, it is believed to have been founded some decades before that by Prince Yaroslav the Wise, hence its name. It served as the capital of the independent principality from 1218 till 1463 when it came under the rule of Moscow. In 1238 it was sacked by the Tartars. In the Time of Troubles the government moved here from Moscow. The Zemsky Sobor ("assembly of the land") composed of representatives of all classes was convened and met in Yaroslavl, it called upon the Russian people to unite and fight against the Polish invaders. In the Time of Troubles when Russia was invaded by the Poles volunteer corps composed of peasants, merchants and noblemen were formed here. Led by Prince Pozharsky and the merchant Minin they defeated the invaders. For its service to the country the city got the right for the tax-free transportation of stone and timber as a result the city rapidly developed and town-planning reached its peak in the 17th century.

The 17th century was the Golden age in the city's history. Lying at the intersection of great trading routes it turned into a bustling commercial centre. Tradesmen from all over the world brought their goods here. Fifty churches from the period testify to the prosperity and piety of its citizens. Fresco painting reached its acme.

Transfiguration Monastery

Kotorosl River, the Volga's tributary

In the bell tower

*Transfiguration Monastery
as viewed from the Kotorosl*

Yaroslavl citizens' gumption was a proverb. The men were usually sober, hardworking, thrifty and strong while the women were very beautiful.

In 1722 one of the earliest and largest textile wills was established here, the rapid growth of textile industry began. In 1750 Feodor Volkov opened the first in Russia drama theatre in Yaroslavl. In 1786 a first provincial newspaper was published here. A rail road between Moscow and Yaroslavl was built in 1870. 1918 was marked by a rebel against the Bolsheviks. In the days of World War II the city gave shelter to the people evacuated from Leningrad which was under siege. Valentina Tereshkova, a native of Yaroslavl, became the first woman cosmonaut, she participated in the *Vostok* space flight in 1963.

Many fine churches survive in the city. Best of them are the churches of St Elijah the Prophet (1647–50), St Nicholas (Nikola Nadein) (1621–22) and the Nativity of Christ (1644). Their interiors are embellished with frescoes. As the painters worked only when it was warm, great mural compositions were executed in one season (from spring till autumn). Yaroslavl icon- and fresco painters were well known all over Russia.

The Transfiguration Monastery used to be the city's religious and cultural centre. Extant within its walls are the churches dating back to the 16th and 17th centuries which are unsurpassed in their beauty. The heart of the ensemble is the Transfiguration Cathedral, the most ancient structure in Yaroslavl: it is almost eight centuries old. *The Song of Igor's Campaign*, a masterpiece of old Russian literature, was found here in the 19th century.

Chapel of St Alexander Nevsky

St Elijah's Church on Central Square

Frescoes in the church. They have never been renovated, only washed

→

Souvenirs made by local craftsmen: painted dishes, dolls, scarves, knitted caps and pictures

KOSTROMA

Kostroma is a city and administrative centre lying at the confluence of the Volga and the Kostroma rivers. Its plants and factories produce excavators, equipment for ships and shoes, other industries are timber working and food procession. Kostroma is a major textile centre, one of the oldest in the country. It is known as the centre of linen production. Sails for ships were once made of its linen, which was Kostroma's contribution to the development of Russian navy.

A good deal of trade went on between Kostroma and the West. Once, so the story goes, a small barrel of gold pieces was found in a shipment of dyes sent from England to the merchant Isakov in exchange for linen goods. A letter was duly dispatched apprising the London company of the discovery. The answer was: "Use the gold for charitable deeds". And so in 1652 Kiril Isakov built the lovely Church of the Resurrection-on-the-Debre in the outskirts of town. This story probably explains why bas-reliefs of the heraldic British lion and unicorn appear on the gate of the church along with the representations of fabulous birds from Russian folklore. The Church of the Resurrection-on-the-Debre is not only the most beautiful of the old buildings in Kostroma, but one of the finest surviving specimens of 17th-century Russian architecture.

Kostroma's population numbers 286.000. It has some higher education institutes: pedagogic, textile and agricultural. There are two theatres, a picture gallery and the local lore museum. It is one of the major tourist sites on the Volga which attracts some 700.000 visitors annually.

It was first mentioned in chronicles in 1214. In 1238 the city was burnt to ashes by the Mongols but soon restored to become an important port and trading centre of the Vladimir principality. Its most

*Holy Trinity Cathedral
in the Ipatiev Monastery*

*Central Square. Fire-observation tower.
Streets radiate out from the square towards
the Volga. A market place is to the left*

Trading arcade of old Kostroma

→
Ipatiev Monastery on the Kostroma River

famous historical place is the Ipatiev Monastery where Prince Mikhail Romanov, the first in the Romanov dynasty, was crowned tsar. His coronation put an end to the troubles and brought peace and order to Russia and prosperity to Kostroma which became the third in importance city in the country, after Moscow and Yaroslavl. Marvellous bright frescoes on the walls of Kostroma's churches are relics of that time. Their colours are well preserved, though the frescoes have never been renovated. In 1773 a larger part of the city was destroyed by a great fire. It took Kostroma 25 years to revive. Peasants from Kostroma had the reputation of being clever, enterprising and of great stature. They travelled on business a lot and knew many things.

The city's original layout has been retained. After the fire of 1773 Kostroma was restored by two architects from St Petersburg who designed its buildings in the style of St Petersburg's Classical ensembles. The city's layout is regular: straight streets radiate out from the central square. The Merchants' Yard (trading arcade) is worth mentioning. It contains passages and galleries named after the kind of foodstuff sold in them: Flour, Fish, Butter and other galleries. Six kilometres away from the centre, on the opposite bank of the river there stands the imposing Ipatiev Monastery crowned with golden cupolas. It is a main architectural landmark and tourist site. The renovated monastery is in a perfect state. Rich historical and art collections are exhibited in the monastery museum.

The Ipatiev Monastery was founded by Boris Godunov's ancestor, a Tartar noblemen converted into Orthodox Christianity, in 1332. Many members of the family were buried within its walls. The Godunovs supported the monastery. It prospered when Boris Godunov ruled the country (1598–1605). After his death Mikhail Romanov was hiding here with his mother Martha who had

Museum of wooden architecture

Palace of Tsar Mikhail Feodorovich

Museum of wooden architecture.
A church transferred from the flooded site

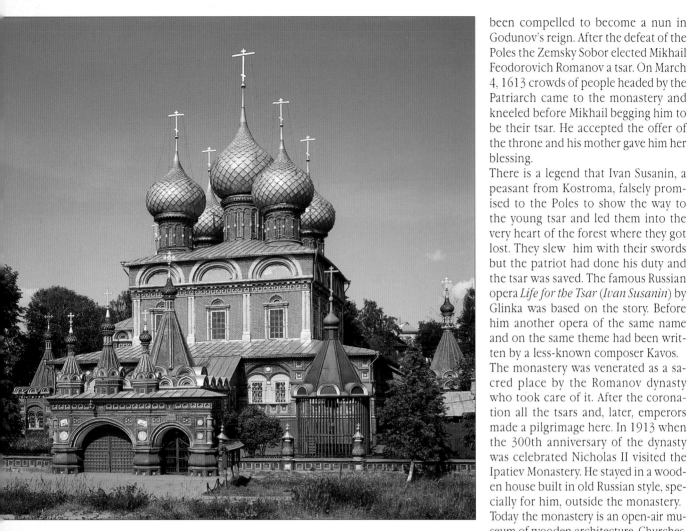

been compelled to become a nun in Godunov's reign. After the defeat of the Poles the Zemsky Sobor elected Mikhail Feodorovich Romanov a tsar. On March 4, 1613 crowds of people headed by the Patriarch came to the monastery and kneeled before Mikhail begging him to be their tsar. He accepted the offer of the throne and his mother gave him her blessing.

There is a legend that Ivan Susanin, a peasant from Kostroma, falsely promised to the Poles to show the way to the young tsar and led them into the very heart of the forest where they got lost. They slew him with their swords but the patriot had done his duty and the tsar was saved. The famous Russian opera *Life for the Tsar (Ivan Susanin)* by Glinka was based on the story. Before him another opera of the same name and on the same theme had been written by a less-known composer Kavos.

The monastery was venerated as a sacred place by the Romanov dynasty who took care of it. After the coronation all the tsars and, later, emperors made a pilgrimage here. In 1913 when the 300th anniversary of the dynasty was celebrated Nicholas II visited the Ipatiev Monastery. He stayed in a wooden house built in old Russian style, specially for him, outside the monastery. Today the monastery is an open-air museum of wooden architecture. Churches, peasants' houses, barns and sheds have been brought from nearby villages and placed here among picturesque groves and small streams.

An exhibition dedicated to the life of Russia's last tsar Nicholas II and his family is displayed on the archbishop's premises.

Leaving Kostroma our ship turns northward and sets off for Moscow.

Resurrection-Church-on-the-Debre

Pavilion on the Volga bank

Kostroma. The Holy Trinity Cathedral

Tutayev (formerly, Romanov) is a town in the Yaroslavl province. It is a river port and railway station. Its industries produce linen, construction materials, foods and sheepskin coats. The population numbers 45.000. The Romanov sheep bred in the 19th century are valued all over Russia for their coarse wool. Coats made of their skin are warm, light and not easily worn out. Such full-length and half-length coats used to be traditional Russian outerwear in winter. The town was once famous for its fast boats, known as the "Romanovs".

It was founded before 1283 by Prince Roman Vladimirovich of Uglich (canonized by the Russian Church) who promoted church construction and donated a lot of money to charity. In his reign 15 churches were built in the town which was, however, named not after him but after another Prince Roman

Vasilyevich of Uglich who constructed here a fortress in 1345.

The most interesting church here is the large and splendid Cathedral of the Resurrection, erected in the 1670s on the foundation of an older 12th-century church.

In 1777 the town was merged with Borisoglebsk and in 1822 changed its name into Romanov-Borisoglebsk. In 1921 it was renamed again, this time into Tutayev, after a Red Army soldier who perished in the Civil War.

*Tutayev (formerly, Romanov-Borisoglebsk).
The Romanov side*

On the Volga bank

*Church of the Kazan Icon
of the Most Holy Theotokos*

The Uglich reservoir was formed by the dam of the Uglich hydroelectric station. Its lake which took the shape in 1939–41 covers 249 km², its volume is 1.25 km³. The reservoir supplies Uglich and its vicinity with water and has good fisheries. Situated in the same area are two smaller old towns: Kaliazin to the south of Uglich and Myshkin to the north, at the entrance to the Rybinsk reservoir. According to legend, the town of Myshkin was founded by a certain Myshkin who built the Dormition Cathedral in Moscow. Another legend tells that a local prince was sleeping on the Volga bank when a mouse chased by a snake woke him up and thus saved from probable death. He ordered to depict the small animal in the town's emblem. In 1877 Myshkin became an administrative centre. This small town with a population of 6.500 has a charm of its own. The fact is that the name of Myshkin is a derivative of "*mysh*" which means "mouse" in Russian. That's why the town boasts the only in the world Museum of Mouse which is a principal tourist attraction. Various objects from all over the world are exhibited there. Representations of mice can be seen everywhere in the town: on pictures, toys and rubbish bins.

Major architectural sights are the cathedrals of St Nicholas (1766) and the Dormition (1820). There is an open-air museum of wooden architecture. Displayed there are 16 wooden structures including houses, barns, smithies, bathhouses etc. The town also has a century-old public library and a picture gallery. Myshkin has a museum of vodka. The famous manufacturer Smirnoff was born in the vicinity.

This horse comes to welcome every ship and is given bread by passengers

Ship in the Uglich lock

Iron gates of the Uglich lock hold the water power

Uglich lock. The water level is increasing and the ship is being raised. Soon the gates will be opened, the ship will pass through them and enter the river

Kaliazin is a river port on the Volga. It was founded in the 12th century at the confluence of the Zhabna and the Volga, on the right bank of the latter. It was originally a small settlement. First references date back to the 15th century when the Holy Trinity Monastery (1473) was established by St Macarius on the lands owned by Kaliaga, whose name was given to the monastery and the town. Ivan the Terrible visited the cloister several times and donated a Gospel to it, now exhibited in a local museum. In 1630 a fortress was built here and in the late 17th century Peter the Great, still a youth, trained his regiments at its walls. In 1775, in the reign of Catherine II, Kaliazin was promoted to the rank of town and had its own emblem. Before 1917 laces made here were very popular. After the construction of the Uglich hydroelectric station in 1937–40 a larger part of Kaliazin was inundated. Its new districts have been built on an elevation.

Today Kaliazin is a relatively small town situated on the Volga in the Tver province. Its population numbers 15.000. It produces *valenky* (traditional Russian felt boots) and linen articles.

We'll see Kaliazin again when sailing along the opposite bank.

Welcome! According to old Russian custom, guests are greeted with bread and salt

While songs are sung, the nation is alive

Leaving the Uglich lock

Motor boats at the canal banks

Waiting

Under sail

Quiet Uglich

Some time ago Arabian coins from the 6th to 9th centuries were excavated on the site of the present Uglich lock, which proved the fact that foreign merchants from the East and Scandinavia as well as Slav tradesmen had called at the port.

Uglich is a town in the Yaroslavl province, a river port and railway station. It produces clocks, watches, cheese and other milk products. Heavy machinery is repaired here. There is a hydroelectric station. The population numbers 39.000. The town has a good museum of art and history. The name of Uglich is a derivative of "ugol" ("a corner"). The Volga makes a sharp bend at this place, forming a corner, or "ugol", hence the name.

Founded as early as 937, it was first mentioned in chronicles only in 1148. A local legend says that the town had existed in the days of Holy Princess Olga, Equal-to-the-Apostles. It served as the capital of the Uglich principality from 1218 till 1238 when it was seized and devastated by the Mongols who killed most of its population. The rest were taken prisoners or fled to the dense forests surrounding the town. In the 14th century Moscow began uniting Russian lands and Uglich was annexed to the Moscow principality. In 1371 it was burnt to ashes by the prince of Tver who struggled with Moscow for supremacy.

In the 15th century the town prospered and even coined its own money. After Ivan the Terrible's death his son, Prince (Tsarevitch) Dimitry, the last in the Rurik dynasty, was sent to Uglich with his mother and killed here, at the age of eight, in 1591 in the uncertain circumstances. His death was not only a tragedy for his family, it was followed by

Transfiguration Cathedral

Interior of St Alexius' Monastery shows the influence of Western architecture

Interior of the Transfiguration Cathedral

Church choir

→
Church of Prince Dimitry the Martyr (Church-on-the-Blood)

many troubles in Russia, such as internecine conflicts and Polish invasion. Three false pretenders to the Muscovite throne (one after another) claimed to be Prince Dimitry. They are known as False Dimitries. Aided by the Lithuanians and the Poles they gathered armies and invaded Russia. That was the Time of Troubles, a period of political crisis in Russia in the early 17th century. *Boris Godunov*, the famous historical tragedy by Alexander Pushkin, was based on the episode from Russian history. Boris Godunov, a favourite of Ivan the Terrible, is presented as the murderer of the boy. The development of the action on two planes, one historical, the other psychological is masterly and is set against background of turbulent events and

Interior of the Transfiguration Cathedral.
Frescoes

Interior of the Church of the Prince Dimitry
the Martyr (Church-on-the-Blood)

Bell sent to Siberia after the death of Prince
Dimitry and returned to Uglich in 1847

ruthless ambitions. Two great operas (by Mussorgsky and Rimsky-Korsakov) were composed on the theme.

In 1606 the prince was canonized and his relics were translated to the Archangel Cathedral in Moscow. In 1611 Uglich was captured by the Poles commanded by Jan Sapieha, who destroyed the town by fire and massacred its population. The chronicle says: "... 20.000 people of all ranks were killed including 500 priests, deacons and church servants. 10 monasteries and 2 convents were destroyed where 2 archimandrites, 8 abbots, 2 abbesses, 500 monks and 500 nuns were murdered. All in all, 40.000 men and women, young and old, rich and poor, were slain, hung, drowned and martyred to death in other ways for their faith in Christ. Remember, o Lord, the departed and grant them rest with the saints in Thine eternal tabernacles".

After the disaster the town restored slowly. The process was hindered by the decree of Peter I forbidding stone construction anywhere in Russia but St Petersburg. The emperor also ordered to remove the bells from the churches of Uglich, melt them and make cannons because Russia was at war with Sweden. In Catherine II's reign the town grew rapidly and flourished. In the 19th century its citizens led tranquil, yet cultured provincial life. A museum, a library and a theatre were opened here. A local teacher wrote a *History of the Town of Uglich* and published it in 1844. In the 1890s Prince Dimitry's palace built in 1462 was renovated and turned into a museum.

The 1917 revolution changed the course of the town's history. It was seriously damaged by construction of the hydroelectric station in the 1930s. The Intercession Monastery, a major architectural sight in the south-western part, and other churches and buildings dating from the 15th, 16th and 17th centuries were exploded and then flooded. The huge and ugly structure of the hydroelectric station stands on the former monastery site today. A team of restorers has been working in the town's

Royal chamber

St Alexius' Monastery

historical centre since 1952. As a result many old buildings have been saved from destruction. According to the plan for Uglich's development and construction, recently approved by the local authorities, its historical centre will be preserved intact.

Main architectural and historical sights include the prince's palace (late 15th century), the Dormition (Miracle) Church and the Resurrection Monastery (17th century). Tourists can also visit St Dimitry's Church-on-the-Blood, the Intercession Church, a royal chamber and other places of interest. Age-old lime-trees grow on the site where the Uglich *kremlin* (fortress) used to be. When Ivan the Terrible besieged the city of Kazan, the *kremlin* walls were dismantled and floated downstream to Kazan where a fortress was built which served the Russian army as a vital stronghold during Kazan's capture.

Today the local authorities try to make the town a popular tourist centre and promote tourist business. The day of

Holy Prince Dimitry the Martyr is celebrated here as the Day of the Protection of Children. Various actions are organized that serve educational purposes, raise money for financial support of mothers and their children and draw the public attention to their problems.

Museum of Russian vodka in Mandroga

Museum of vodka in Uglich

*Russian Log Cabin,
a vodka-tasting bar in Uglich*

Invitation to taste vodka

Devices for refining vodka

*Best sorts of vodka, winners
of international competitions*

Only vodka from Russia – is genuine Russian vodka!

Let's take a look at Kaliazin from the opposite bank. After the confluence with the River Kashinka the Volga turns to the right and a striking view opens out before our eyes... In the middle of the river the tall bell-tower of St Nicholas' Cathedral (built in 1800) rises high above its smooth surface. The cathedral used to stand in a bustling square of the cosy town. Its clean streets with small two-storey houses and gardens in blossom led to the trading arcade, a usual feature in provincial towns. It was a busy trading and handicraft quarter whose inhabitants were occupied with gardening and crafts, made felt and leather boots. In 1753 the settlement was promoted to the rank of town. In the late 19th century Kaliazin had a weaving mill, a food procession plant, shipyards and smithies. Its male population floated rafts down the Volga while women were skilled in spinning, weaving and making laces. The town was prosperous. Ships stopped here and various goods were carried from Kaliazin downstream, their total weight was more than 800.000 *pouds* (13.200 tons). Brought to the town were flour, wheat, rye, salt and starch (total weight 16.000 tons). A larger part of the town was flooded in 1940, after the construction of the Uglich reservoir which increased the water elevation up to 12 m for 50 km behind the dam. The Trinity Monastery was covered with water, only some buildings standing on the hills have been preserved, including stone houses dating from the 18th and 19th centuries and the Ascension Church (1787).

The bell tower sticking up out of the water is an ominous sight, a relic of the past and a sort of navigation mark for ships.

Kaliazin. Bell tower of St Nicholas' Cathedral-on-the-Zhabna. This part of the town has been flooded after the construction of the Uglich lock

In the morning

Unruffled water surface

...and quiet low banks

The Moscow Canal (formerly, the Moskva-Volga Canal) joins these two famous Russian rivers – the Volga and the Moskva. Construction of the Volga-Don and Volga-Baltic waterways has opened up the capital of Russia situated in the very centre of the continent to five seas: the White, Baltic, Black, Azov and Caspian. The idea of joining the Volga and the Moskva rivers dates back from the 18th century. Peter I dreamt of building a canal to connect the Baltic Sea through the Volga and the Moskva rivers with Central Russia. His plan was not realized then. It was done much later when the problem of supplying Moscow with water arose in the early 20th century. The canal's construction took an unusually short time (from 1932 till 1937). In the period of four years and eight months 8 hydroelectric stations (the largest of them is at Ivankovo), 11 locks, 5 pumping plants, 11 dams, 19 bridges, 2 tunnels and lots of other special structures were built, which was an immense work. The canal is 128 km long, of which 19 km are taken up by reservoirs. To estimate the scale of the construction we can compare the Moscow Canal with other longest canals in the world: the White Sea – Baltic Canal is 227 km long, the Volga-Don Canal 101 km long, the Suez Canal 161 km long, the Kiel Canal 99 km long and the Panama Canal 65 km long. If all the earth dug out during the construction had been put into freight trains, they would have formed a line 5.5 times longer than the equator.

The canal was mainly built by political prisoners who worked in terrible conditions so the expenses were minimal. In 1947 when the capital of Russia was celebrating its 800th anniversary and the canal its 10th anniversary it was named after Moscow.

It serves various purposes. Historically plagued by short water supply, Moscow by the 1930s urgently needed linking to a major water source. Well water utilized in the 1700s had long dried up; spring water used in the 1800s had also been exhausted. A 1904 pipeline to the Moscow River provided relief for only about 25 years, after which time the river became so depleted that it could be crossed on foot in front of the Kremlin. The canal supplies Moscow with Volga water which is purified at pumping plants. Moscow uses more water than other world capitals. The canal made the water level in the Moskva River much higher which has increased the navigation and new ports have been opened in Khimki (the Northern Port of Moscow) and Dmitrov. The banks of the canal and reservoirs are a popular pleasure resort of Muscovites.

Moscow Canal. Locking

Moscow Canal. The Dmitrov lock

Dormition Cathedral

*Newly built church in Dmitrov.
The Russians return to the Christian faith*

Moscow Canal. The lock No 6

Bon voyage!

Following the Moscow Canal our ship puts into the Khimki reservoir built in 1937 on the delta of the Khimka River. It covers 3.5 km², the maximum depth is 18 m. The difference in the water elevations in the reservoir and the Moskva is 36 m. The reservoir is located within the city boundaries.

The River Khimka has given its name not only to the reservoir but also to the town of Khimki in the vicinity of Moscow which used to be a post station in the road from Moscow to Tver and Novgorod the Great. Many celebrated figures of Russian culture visited those parts. The composer Tchaikovsky, the writer Kuprin, the painter Levitan, the founder of the gallery of his name Tretyakov, the theatre producer Stanislavsky and many others spent their holidays there.

The Northern River Port is situated on the reservoir bank. It was built in 1937 and reconstructed in 1974. The total length of its quays is 2.2 km. It is a place of destination for numerous slow barges loaded with sand, gravel and other construction materials.

Next to the port stands the Northern River Station. It was opened in 1937, simultaneously with the canal. The building is one of Moscow's architectural sights. Made of granite and marble and embellished with arcades and galleries it is elegant and graceful. It has the shape of a double-deck river steamer used in the early 20th century. The tower in the middle looks like a navigating bridge and its high steel spire crowned with a star is like a mast. A wide staircase descends from the central portal to the landing stage (its total length is 1.5 km). Comfortable liners start from here on long voyages to Astrakhan, Rostov-on-Don and St Petersburg. An open gallery supported by 150 four-edged columns of white stone runs along the perimeter on its ground floor. The building of the station is 150 m long and its spire is 85 m high. In the territory round the station there used to be grasslands fringed with docks where cows were pastured. A large park covering 50 hectares has been laid out here.

The design of the Northern River Station was made in accordance with the official ideology of the early Soviet period expressing the optimism and enthusiasm of the masses. This tendency is evident in many Moscow's buildings. The sumptuous and imposing decor of the station combines architecture, sculpture and painting and conveys the elevated and triumphant mood of the first socialist "five-year periods".

From the river station we start our sight-seeing tour round Moscow.

Moscow. The Northern River Station

*Facade decoration
of the Northern River Station*

*Statue symbolizing the Moscow Canal
at the entrance to the river station*

Moscow

For centuries Moscow has been a treasure house of carefully preserved national tradition. All the Russian tsars and emperors were crowned here in Russia's main cathedral, the ancient Dormition Cathedral, and both Peter the Great and Catherine the Great came to Moscow to celebrate their military victories. In 1812 the city was a sacrifice on the altar of the war, yet precipitated the inglorious demise of Napoleon's great army. In May 1945 it greeted the victorious Russian troops coming back from Germany.

Moscow has changed greatly! You'll see other sights, different from those of the past. Still there is something eternal and everlasting in its look. History is alive in it and we can't forget it.

Excavations in the Kremlin have testified to the fact that a settlement existed on the site in the ancient time. In the 12th century there were some villages owned by a boyar Kuchka. Arabian coins from the 9th century found in the former market place prove that, even before that, there had been a settlement here, at the intersection of trading routes connecting the north and the south. Some scholars consider the name of Moscow a derivation from the language of the *Meri* tribe. In this dead language the word group "moskh akva" means "a bear". There are, however, other interpretations of the name. Moscow was first mentioned in chronicles in 1147, although archaeological evidence shows that a Slav settlement has existed on the site since the 6th century. Yury Dolgoruky is considered Moscow's founder. In 1156 he built the first fortifications – ditches and earthen ramparts topped by a wooden wall. That was the Kremlin. In 1237 Moscow shared the fate of other Russian towns. Like all the towns of the Vladimir-Suzdal principality it was captured and burnt by the Mongols. In 1326 the Metropolitan of

Panoramic view of Moscow's centre

Kremlin as viewed from the Moskva River

Cathedral of Christ the Saviour

→
Red Square

the Russian Orthodox Church transferred his seat from Vladimir to Moscow. In the 13th century Moscow grew in importance, in the 14th century became the capital of the principality and in the second half of the 15th century the capital of the united Russian state. In 1380 Prince Dimitry of Moscow with the blessing of St Sergius of Radonezh inflicted a crushing defeat on the Mongols at Kulikovo on the Don River for which victory he was thereafter known as Dimitry Donskoy (of the Don). Two years later the Golden Horde attacked and burnt the city in revenge. In 1453 after the fall of Constantinople Moscow declared itself "the third Rome". In 1517 the Crimean Tartars destroyed and burnt the city again. In the mid-16th century Ivan the Terrible conquered the Tartar khanates of Kazan and Astrakhan and annexed them to Moscow. In 1612 the Russian army and volunteers under the energetic leadership of Prince Pozharsky and the merchant Minin forced the Poles who had seized Moscow to surrender.

After Peter I had transferred the capital to St Petersburg and compelled the court and the government to move there, Moscow retained its major role in the life of Russia, it was still the country's heart, Russian emperors were crowned here. Its rivalry with St Petersburg in the spheres of art, literature and science was fruitful. Its holy places (churches and monasteries) were greatly venerated and attracted pilgrims. In the autumn of 1812 it was occupied by Napoleon. A fire broke out and spread rapidly. Looting was rife. The lack of supplies and shelter made it impossible for Napoleon to winter in Moscow. After the victory over Napoleon and after the catastrophic retreat of the French troops Moscow was rapidly restored and rebuilt. In 1817 a new plan for the development of the ancient capital was introduced by the specially organized Construction Committee. It launched a great program of rebuilding, which included a partial replanning of the city centre.

After a fierce fighting for five days in November, 1917, the Bolshevik power was firmly established in Moscow. In March 1918 the Soviet government moved to the city which resumed its former status as capital. The status was ratified on December 30, 1922 when the Union of the Soviet Socialist Republics was set up. In the 1930s Moscow was re-planned and rebuilt on a large scale. Old streets were replaced with wide modern avenues and the city's layout changed. The Moscow metro, one of the deepest and most comfortable in the world, was built. The historical centre of the city was greatly damaged: old narrow streets with cosy houses disappeared forever, many churches, monasteries and other monuments were destroyed, the majestic Cathedral of Christ the Saviour, a memorial to the Russian victory over Napoleon, was demolished. It has been recently restored on its original site.

During World War II (1941–45) Moscow suffered a great deal. On December 6, 1941 a desperate counterattack threw the Germans back from the outskirts and saved Moscow. That was the first defeat of the Nazis. The Russian army moved 350 km westward. After the war recovery was quick and followed by further construction of new districts and annexation of outskirts and suburbs. Moscow with its satellites (outer Moscow) covers 1.000 km².

Most important international conferences and festivals are held here. In 1980 Moscow was the host for the Olympic Games. It is the largest industrial centre of Russia. Its main industries are engineering and metalworking. Textile industry has been traditional here. Moscow used to be called not only a "white-stoned", "golden-domed" and

Annunciation Cathedral

Saviour Tower with the famous clock: the Kremlin chimes

Golden-domed city of Moscow

Terem Palace

Easter egg decorated with the portraits of Russian tsars and emperors. Carl Faberge's firm. The State Armoury

Sheathed sabre. The State Armoury

Royal regalia (crowns, sceptre and globe, an order of St Andrew the First-Called). The Russian Diamond Fund

"hospitable" city but also the centre of printed cotton production. Hosts of books and works of art are dedicated to Moscow. In the Soviet period it played an important international role as the capital of the multinational state. There are many popular songs about Moscow.

Moscow is a major tourist and business centre. Many comfortable hotels coming up to the highest standards have recently been erected here. The *Cosmos* hotel ranks among the hotels of the first international class. The building was designed by Russian and French architects and engineers and constructed by a French firm. The upper part of its very tall structure comprising twenty-seven storeys has the shape of a semi-cylinder. After the reconstruction the *Balchug* hotel has turned into a hotel of high European standard. The range of services provided and comfortableness put it among the most famous hotels of the world. The *Renaissance* and *President* are also de luxe hotels. The *Metropol* hotel designed in

the Art Nouveau style is to be found in the city centre in Theatre Square. Its plain facades are rather impressive. The upper floors are crowned with a big sculptured frieze and a ceramic panel *Princesse Reverie* by Mikhail Vrubel. The sophisticated silhouette of the top part forms the smooth line of the roof against the blue sky.

Moscow is a major scientific and cultural centre. In 1934 the Academy of Science was transferred here from St Petersburg (Leningrad). The city has numerous research and higher education institutes. Its main museums are the State Museum of History, the Armoury Palace in the Kremlin, the Pushkin Museum of Fine Arts, the Tretyakov Gallery, the Polytechnic Museum, Bakhrushin's Museum of Theatre and many others. It boasts fine architectural ensembles including the Kremlin, the Donskoy and St Simon monasteries, the Novodevichy Convent and St Daniel's Monastery, the residence of the Patriarch of Moscow and All Russia who is the head of the Russian Orthodox Church. Moscow is the seat of the President and the government. The Federal Assembly consisting of two chambers, the State Duma and the Council of Federation, has its sessions here.

In 1997 Moscow celebrated its 850th anniversary. It would take a whole life to see all of the Russian metropolis which has 25.000 historical and cultural sights and monuments, 70 museums, 50 theatres, 125 cinemas, 4.500 libraries and 540 research and higher education institutes. The city is famous not only for its palaces, parks, monumental sculpture, modern thoroughfares and wide avenues but also for the numerous old streets, lanes, alleys and cul-de-sacs (blind alleys), so typical of it. Their centuries-old euphonious names should be preserved as carefully as are the palaces, parks and other historical sights.

When we see Moscow we can't but remember the words of the famous playwright Griboyedov: "There is no other city like Moscow". Where should we go after the sightseeing tour round the capital of Russia which is sure to prove incomplete. Let's return to St Petersburg and see the familiar route from Moscow to St Petersburg from a new angle. The city is much younger than Moscow. It is preparing for the celebration of its 300th anniversary, yet it is as inexhaustible as the old capital and we will be pleased to see it again...

Metropol *hotel*

Bolshoy Opera and Ballet Theatre

State Tretyakov Gallery

Exhibition of National Economic Achievements. The Friendship of the Peoples *fountain*

Moscow at night. One of Moscow's sky-scrapers

RUSSIAN RIVER CRUISE

English edition

Ivan Fiodorov Art Publishers
11 Zvenigorodskaya St
191119, St Petersburg, Russia

Ivan Fiodorov Printing Company,
St Petersburg (1917)

ISBN 5-93893-154-1

Printed and bound in Russia